WHAT ARE THIS MAN'S SECRETS?*

How does George Burns do it?

And just what does he do?

Now at last America's #1 sex symbol (such infants as Tom Selleck and Richard Gere simply don't count) gives you his very special formula for a long and very lively life (plus how to make a good martini).

You don't have to be over 85 to be as wonderfully wise and outrageously funny as George Burns. On the other hand, it certainly helps if you want to write a book called—

How to Live to Be 100—Or More:

*Hint: On the eighth day, George Burns created God.

How to Live to Be 100—Or More: The Ultimate Diet, Sex and Exercise Book*

* At My Age, Sex Gets Second Billing

How to Live to Be 100 —Or More: The Ultimate Diet, Sex and Exercise Book*

GEORGE BURNS

*At My Age, Sex Gets Second Billing

A SIGNET BOOK
NEW AMERICAN LIBRARY

SIGNET TRADEMARK REG. U.S. PAT. OFF. AND FOREIGN COUNTRIES
REGISTERED TRADEMARK—MARCA REGISTRADA
HECHO EN CHICAGO, U.S.A.

THIS BOOK *is dedicated to the widows of my last six doctors.*

Contents

If You Bought the Book, Start Here; If Not, Put It Back

WELL, I'm going to write another book. This is my fourth one, and I've learned that the most important thing about writing a book is to have a great first chapter to grab your readers. If you've got that, from then on everything flows. I've also learned that writing a first chapter is not easy. I've been sitting here for three hours and nothing's happened. So I'm going to make this my second chapter.

If this were Chapter One, I'd tell you how this whole book came about. But this is Chapter Two, not Chapter One, and it doesn't belong in Chapter Two. On the other hand, how can I not tell you readers how this whole thing got started? Maybe I better skip Chapter Two and go to Chapter Three. The way I'm going, I may finish this book before I get to the end of the page.

Anyway, I know you're dying of curiosity, so

Author at work

here's how it started. My publisher called and said, "George, we want you to write a book, and we've got a great title for it: 'How to Live to Be 100—Or More'!"

I said, "I don't like that title. How about 'If I Can Do It, You Can Do It'?"

She said, "Too vague. What's wrong with 'How to Live to Be 100—Or More'?"

"How about 'The George Burns Health and Exercise Book'?"

"Dull."

"Then how about 'Long Life Is a Many-Splendored Thing'?"

"You've got to be kidding."

Then I said, "How about—"

Interrupting, she said, "Look, George, you're getting a very big advance—do you want to write this book or don't you?"

"How about 'How to Live to Be 100—Or More'?" I asked.

"George, you just came up with a great title!"

"Thank you," I said.

There's nothing like having a publisher with an open mind.

Now, you're probably asking why would anyone want to live to be 100. I'll tell you, but first I should mention that parts of this book will be funny and parts will be serious. I just hope you can tell which is which. But don't worry—when it gets really serious I'll let you know.

Now, what was that question? Oh yeah—why would anyone want to live to be 100? I know some people who are not the least interested in reaching that age, but it so happens they're all under 10. What do they care about growing old? They've got more important things to worry about, like whether the cookies are crisp. Most of the people I know who are still living want to keep living. I'm a member of the Hillcrest Country Club, and I must run into fifty or sixty people a day. I've yet to meet anybody who said, "George, I'd like to die today." Dying is not popular; it's never caught on. That's understandable; it's bad for the complexion. It also upsets your daily routine and leaves you with too much time on your hands.

Believe me, the urge to live is very powerful. It goes way back to Adam and Eve, who by the way, started another very popular urge. We're very lucky. We probably wouldn't be here if Adam had enjoyed the apple instead.

I don't know about you, but there are lots of reasons for me to live to be 100 or more. For one thing, I've got all these age jokes and I've got to use them—they're funny. Like when I talk about becoming a country singer and I say, "Why shouldn't I be a country singer? I'm older than most countries."

That gets a laugh. Or I'll say, "They had this song, 'I Wish I Was 18 Again,' and they wanted the oldest man around to sing it. But at that time Moses happened to be booked so they asked me." That's another laugh.

Now Bob Hope, Milton Berle, and Alan King can't do that kind of material. Those kids are too young. I found out that with an age joke the older I get, the bigger the laugh. When I'm 100 I'll be getting screams.

Whoever handled Methuselah sure blew it. The old boy lived to be 969. He'd have made a fortune in show business. Too bad—I could have used some of his stuff.

Age jokes never miss. Well, almost never. Recently I played a college, and after the show some of the kids came back to see me. They asked me different questions, and one kid wanted to know if I really started out as a dancer.

I told him I had. Then I thought I would throw in a little age joke. I said, "One time I asked Betsy Ross to go out dancing, but she couldn't—she was busy sewing something."

The kids just stared at me. Now to most people that would be funny because it means I was around when Betsy Ross was, and also that I was too dumb to know she was sewing the flag. Well, one of the kids stopped staring and asked me if Betsy Ross was a good dancer. Another wanted to know why Betsy Ross couldn't have stopped sewing, danced with me, and then started sewing again. A third thought Betsy Ross was Diana Ross's sister, and the fourth said, "Who's Diana Ross?"

That's when I said, "Kids, the interview is over." I don't mind laying an egg on the stage, but not in my dressing room.

As I said, there are a lot of reasons why I want to live to be 100 or more. And I'm sure you all have your reasons, too, or you'd be reading *Penthouse*. Come to think of it, that can kill you faster than anything else. I'm sure a lot of you men are ready to stick around as long as it takes to keep your wives from collecting on your insurance.

I personally know Mickey Rooney's reason. He has to live to 100 so he can pay the alimony he owes all those ex-wives. He's not allowed to die.

Dean Martin's a cinch to make it, he's already 80-proof. If he does go, he won't go alone. He'll take his old friend Jack Daniels with him.

And then there's Phyllis Diller. Her face-lifts alone will hold her up until she's past 100. Besides, she doesn't want her husband, Fang, to collect on her insurance.

Well, here I am at the end of Chapter One, Two or Three, and now I'm ready to get to the important question. How do you do it?—How do you live to be 100 or more? There are certain things you have to do. The most important one is you have to be sure to make it to 99. See, I told you I'd get serious.

Exercise Can Do Wonders:
Look at Me, But Not Too Closely

PEOPLE KEEP ASKING me, "George, you're 87, how do you do it? You make pictures, you do television, you give concerts, you record albums, smoke cigars, drink martinis, you go out with pretty girls—how do you do it?"

It's very simple. For instance, a martini. You fill the glass with ice, then you pour in some gin and a touch of vermouth, add an olive, and you've got yourself a martini.

I also do exercises and walk a lot. And walking is even easier than making a martini. I take one foot and put it in front of the other foot, then I take the other foot and put it in front of the other foot, and before I know it I'm walking. And you don't even need an olive.

Most people agree that walking is good for your health. And yet where I live in Beverly Hills nobody walks. If they have to go three blocks, they drive.

Some people even have two, three, or four cars. I've got one neighbor who has a little car to drive to his big car.

Now me, every morning I get up and go out in my backyard, and rain or shine I walk for a mile and a half. Well, that's not quite true—I'm exaggerating. If it rains, I let Gene Kelly do the walking. But I don't let him sing. Around my house I do the singing.

I've got a regular routine. I walk through the yard, around the pool, through the trees and back to where I started. And I do this forty times. That covers the mile and a half. Oh, I must tell you— one morning when I was filming the *Oh God!* movie, I got carried away with the part I played. Instead of going around the pool I tried to walk across it. Swimming is a good exercise, too.

My advice is to walk whenever you can. It's free, costs nothing, and it not only makes you live longer and feel better, but it also keeps you looking trim. To me that's important. I've always been very conscious of my body. I'm conscious of the fact that it doesn't look like Burt Reynolds's. And he's probably conscious of the fact that his doesn't look like mine. But that's his problem. If he wants to look better, let him get out there in the rain with Gene Kelly.

But, like anything else, you can overdo walking, too. A friend of mine from Beverly Hills has been walking five miles a day for six months. He called me last week and told me he was just passing through Vancouver and would I like him to send me some canned salmon.

Now, for those who find walking boring, golf can be the answer. It's a great game and you're out in the open air. The only trouble is, at the club I belong to, the golfers do very little walking; most of them drive around in carts. The members look lousy and the caddies look great.

If you want to live to be 100 or older, you can't just sit around waiting for it to happen. You have to get up each day and go after it. We're talking here about perhaps the most important key to longevity. Besides walking, I have a whole program of exercises that I do every day. There are many different exercise programs with many different objectives. Mine is to keep me limber, toned up, and feeling good. Look, I'm not trying to get any taller or build up a lot of big muscles I can't use. Somebody told me all those big muscles make you top-heavy and you fall down a lot. Well, he's wrong, too. I've yet to see Dolly Parton fall down.

Anyway, this is my exercise program. It takes about a half hour, and I do it every morning before breakfast. As you'll see, the first five exercises I do lying flat on my back on the floor:

No. 1—Rump Raiser

(A great way to start the day. Get it out of bed and get it off the floor.)

This is also good for stretching the lower part of your back. Heels together, knees bent and legs apart. Using back for support, raise your rear end off the floor as high as possible, then lower it. I repeat this 25 times.

I suggest you work up to it gradually unless you want to learn to live on the floor.

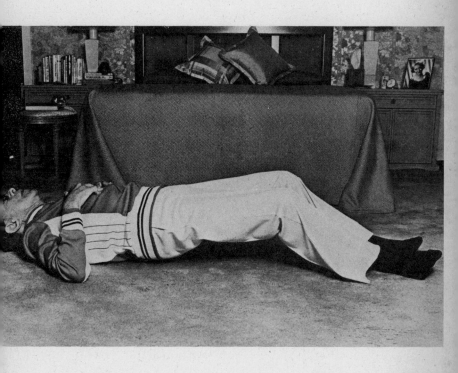

No. 2—The Knee-Hi

(I named this exercise after a Chinese girl I used to dance with.)

This is good for stretching muscles in the thigh and hip. Interlock fingers and grasp one knee. Keeping other leg straight, pull knee up as far as possible, trying to reach chin. Alternate knees, which should be easy if you have two of them. I do this 10 times for each knee.

No. 3—The Pedal Pusher

Hands on chest, legs in the air, make believe you're riding a bicycle. I pedal 100 times.

Of course, if you have a bicycle, skip this and go to the next exercise.

No. 4—The Sit-Up

(You may notice I'm not alone. But to hold your interest and also mine, I thought we'd improve the scenery.)

There are many versions of the Sit-Up. But being an old-fashioned sentimentalist, I prefer the basic Sit-Up. Hands in back of head, legs straight, bring yourself to a sitting position. In sitting position stretch forward two or three times, then return to prone position. I do this 15 times.

This is not an easy exercise, but it's very rewarding. Look what it's done for her.

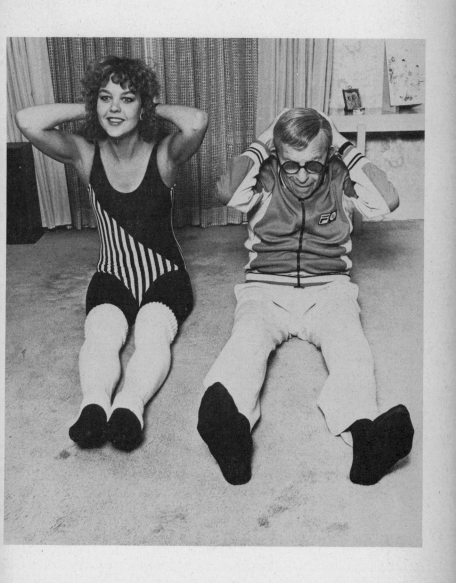

No. 5—Bottoms Up

(This is not a toast, it's an exercise.)

Hands stretched on floor at your sides, throw both legs over your head and try to touch floor in back of you with your toes. I do this 10 times.

I must admit I can't touch the floor, but I go as far as I can. Of course, I'm referring to the exercise.

No. 6—The Yoga

(It's not really a yoga position, but let them sue me. You'll notice I have changed girls. I had to, they can't keep up with me.)

Sitting position on floor, knees spread apart as far as possible. Bring the feet together so soles touch each other. Hold on to toes, pull body forward as far as you can, and return to first position. I do this 25 times.

I like this exercise. It makes me feel like I'm taking bows.

No. 7—The Neck Stretcher

(The name of this exercise came to me one morning while I was stretching my neck. You can see, the girl isn't with me. This exercise takes place on my bed, and I felt I should protect her reputation.)

Sit on edge of bed. Turn head to right and stretch as far as you can. Then do same thing to left. I repeat this 5 times. Then stretch head up and stretch it down. I repeat this 5 times.

Then roll head in circle five times, then do same thing in reverse direction.

This exercise keeps your neck limber and does away with a double chin. I'm not sure that's true, because I've never had a double chin. But then again, maybe that's why.

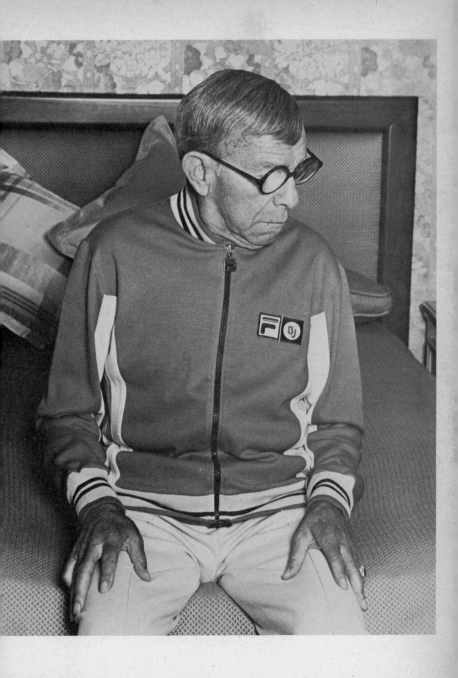

No. 8—The Front Bender

(This exercise has been around for hundreds of years. I like it. I like anything that's older than I am. And you'll notice I like things younger than I am, too.)

Standing erect, raise hands high overhead. Keeping knees straight, bend over and touch floor. I do this 15 times. When you first start out you may not be able to touch the floor. But don't worry, I won't tell Jack LaLanne.

No. 9—The Side Bender

(How about that. Two benders in a row without a martini.)

Stand erect, keeping legs straight, hips forward, hands on hips. From waist up bend to left as far as you can, then repeat to the right. I do this 40 times. But remember, I count left and right as only 1. Otherwise, it would be 80 times.

    If you don't like this exercise, go back to Bottoms Up.

No. 10—The Finale

(Otherwise known as the last exercise.)

Stand with feet slightly apart. Twist body as far as you can to the left, then repeat to the right. I do this 40 times. And that's it.

 These exercises take me about half an hour, as I told you in the beginning; that is, unless I get a phone call from that friend of mine walking through Vancouver. Then it might take me an hour and thirty-two minutes.

(This is not an exercise, but it makes me feel just as good . . . maybe better.)

Worry, Stress, and Tension: Don't Take Them to Bed With You

IF YOU ASK ME what is the single-most important key to longevity, I would have to say it is avoiding worry, stress, and tension. And if you didn't ask me, I'd still have to say it.

I know I've already said that exercise is the most important key to longevity, but that was when I was writing the exercise chapter. When I get around to the chapter on sex I'll make that the most important. That's the way I write. Look, Hemingway had his faults, I've got mine.

Now, let's see if I know what I'm talking about. What is the difference between worry, stress, and tension? I really don't know. They're not exactly the same. They overlap and run into each other. Worry leads to stress, and stress leads to tension. You can't have one without the other, which is a song I sang when I played the Colonial Theatre in Schenectady on the same bill with Worry, Stress & Tension. See how it all ties together?

Okay, what are some of the things people worry about these days? Well—they're afraid the world will be blown up; crime on the streets and in their homes; overpopulation; gray hair; wrinkles; traffic congestion; parking tickets; marriage; divorce; houseguests; medical bills; inflation; flying saucers; too much salt, too much sugar; too much chlorine in the water, not enough chlorine in the water. . . . I could go on and on, and I think I will . . . there's depression; unemployment; sharks . . . that's enough.

It's not that there haven't always been things to worry about, but when there were just newspapers we weren't aware of them as much. Radio and television have brought them right into our homes. At four o'clock in the afternoon the news starts, and from then until 7:30 all you see are explosions, wars, fires, murders, crashes. . . . You very seldom see a cute little Girl Scout selling cookies. I love cookies; I hate sharks. And in case you start feeling good again, along comes the 11 o'clock news with a rerun of the whole thing, so you'll be sure to get a good night's sleep.

I don't know about you, but the way I figure, I can't change the world, but I can change the channel. Which is exactly what I did last night. What do you think I got? Bela Lugosi biting three beautiful girls on their necks. It scared the hell out of me. I switched back to the news, watched a half hour of it, and slept like a baby.

Let's get serious for a moment. Worry, stress, and tension are not only unpleasant, but they can shorten your life. When your body is under stress it manufactures certain chemicals that poison your whole system, lower your resistance, and raise your blood pressure. And we all know that high blood pressure is the major cause of strokes and heart attacks.

Well, the serious moment is over, it's time for a tension breaker. Turn the page.

(For men. Ladies see opposite page.)

(Photograph by Vera Anderson.)

Well, back to worry, stress, and tension. They come in all sizes. Some people are bothered by big things, others are bothered by little things. That's because to some people the big things are the little things, and the little things are the big things. We'll talk more about that on the chapter dealing with sex.

The closest friend I ever had was Jack Benny. He was gentle, kind, beautiful . . . I loved him. But Jack was one of those people whom little things bothered. Big things never fazed him. One day he was having lunch at our club, and that very day he had just signed a three-million-dollar contract. I knew about it, so I walked over to congratulate him. But he looked very depressed.

I said, "Jack, is anything wrong?"

"Yeah, my coffee isn't hot," he answered.

"Is that why you're upset?"

"How can they serve lukewarm coffee?" he exclaimed.

"Jack, you just signed a three-million-dollar contract."

He glared at me and said, "That doesn't make the coffee any hotter!"

That was Tuesday. On Thursday the television ratings came out, and Jack's show had dropped six points. Now you all know what the ratings mean in our business. If you drop one point, you want to kill yourself.

There was Jack having lunch again. I was afraid to go over, but I figured I was his friend so I should console him. I went up to him, but instead of being dejected he had a big smile on his face. . . . I don't think I have to finish this story. You're right, his coffee was hot.

Jack was amazing. He played the Palace in New York seven or eight times a year, the Palladium in London numerous times, and all the big theaters and night clubs. On the stage Jack was calm, cool, and confident; he never thought for a second that he wouldn't do well. But the minute he and Mary gave a party he was a nervous wreck. Which means Jack was nervous once every twelve years. That's not true—Jack and Mary gave a lot of parties, and they were always great. But Jack constantly worried that his guests weren't having a good time.

I remember one party, there must have been 150 people there, and we were all having a fine time, talking and drinking and laughing—all except Jack. He called me aside and said, "George, the party's not moving."

I said, "Jack, it's moving. Everybody's having a wonderful time."

"Stop buttering me up," he said. "I'm in show business, too, you know. I've played for audiences all my life, and this party is just lying there!"

I said, "Jack, you want this party to really

move? Go upstairs, take off your pants, put on one of Mary's hats, and come down in your shorts playing the violin."

You won't believe this. He said, "Great idea," and up he went.

I turned to the guests, and in a hushed voice called for attention. "Ladies and gentlemen, our host, Mr. Jack Benny, star of stage, screen, and television, has gone upstairs and will be coming down in his shorts wearing a lady's hat and playing his violin. Just ignore him."

Down came our star doing his act, and nobody paid any attention to him. It finally dawned on Jack that I had been putting him on. He fell on the floor laughing, everyone else laughed, the party was a smash, and Jack was happy—until the next party.

That was Jack. He didn't worry about television ratings or signing million-dollar contracts—he worried that the towels wouldn't be fluffy enough when he took a shower.

I've always been lucky. Little things never bothered me. I didn't care how fluffy Jack's towels were when he took a shower. It was a long time before I knew what worry, stress, and tension meant. I couldn't even spell them. I only went as far as the fourth grade. In fact, I was in the fourth grade so long I finally got too old to take out my teacher, Miss Hollander.

I came from a very poor family; seven sisters and four brothers, and we had nothing. And when you've got nothing, there's nothing to lose. So there's nothing to worry about. That's the way it was in our neighborhood. Everybody had nothing to lose.

When I was 7 years old I told my mother I was going into show business. Three other kids and I were going to call ourselves the Peewee Quartet. She said, "That doesn't make sense. You're making around eighty-five cents a week selling newspapers, crackers . . . shining shoes . . . and you want to give up all that to go into show business?"

I told my mother, "You know how I love to sing, it's something inside of me that has to come out."

She said, "When you're singing in the house around your brothers and sisters, that's one thing. But when you're singing in front of strangers and it comes out, they'll push it back in again."

You might not laugh at that, but I did. My mother had a very funny delivery.

Well, I went into show business and stayed there. And my mother was right. For the next twenty years the audience kept pushing it back. In those days the most popular form of entertainment was vaudeville. There was the B. F. Keith Circuit, the Orpheum, the Moss & Brill, the Loew's, the

Pantages, the Gus Sun, etc., and if you played any of these circuits, you were a success. And that meant you had a lot to worry about. If the audience didn't laugh in the right spots, or cry in the right spots, or applaud, you could get canceled. Even great performers would worry—performers like Al Jolson; Eddie Cantor; Clayton, Jackson and Durante; Jack Benny; Milton Berle; Sophie Tucker; Smith and Dale; Eva Tanguay; Belle Baker; Block and Sully; the Marx Bros.; the Gliding O'Mearas; Madam Burkhart and her Cockatoos; Power's Elephants; Swain's Cats and Rats—they were all nervous. They'd lie awake worrying. But not me. I never missed a night's sleep. Why would I? I wasn't playing those good theaters.

I played theaters that were so broken down, if they canceled me, they would have been doing me a favor. Let me tell you a story. When I was about 18 I was working alone, and I was booked to play the Myrtle Theater in Brooklyn. Now, the show started at 1:00 o'clock, but you rehearsed your music at ten. Well, the manager heard my rehearsal, and I was canceled. I was the only actor in show business who was canceled before he opened. I got so used to being canceled, I asked for more money. I figured as long as I was laying off, why not lay off from a better-paying job?

I finally started playing some good theaters, but

I still didn't worry, because by then I realized I had a big talent. And I was married to her for thirty-eight years.

In 1932 Gracie and I got our first radio show. It was a whole new thing for us, but I didn't let that worry me either. And we were always in the Top Ten. We had to be—there were only eight shows. Then came the transition to television. I was starting to get a little nervous about that, but then I thought, what's the big deal? I had talked to an audience in vaudeville, in radio I talked to a microphone, so now I was talking to a camera. If you have to worry about talking, you're in big trouble.

My attitude is, if something is beyond your control—if you can't do anything about it—there's no point worrying about it. And if you can do something about it, then there's still nothing to worry about. I feel that way when the plane I'm on is bouncing around in turbulence. It's not my problem. The pilot gets a lot of money to fly that plane; let him worry about it. True, I never fly in those small, private planes, but that's for a different reason. If I'm going down, I want to have an audience with me.

I can honestly say I was not even uptight about my heart bypass several years ago. I don't mean to minimize that operation—I would have preferred to have had my cuticles cut—but once again, what could I do about it? It was beyond my control. It was the doctor's business; that's what he does for a living. Me, I'm a country singer. Besides, the surgeon had trained for years in medical school, he'd done this operation many times . . . and he had long, strong fingers. I had such confidence in him that I didn't give it a second thought.

When I came out of the anesthetic I heard the surgeon say, "George, you did great, you're just fine."

I said, "Doctor, I wasn't the least bit concerned."

"Really?" he said. "I was a nervous wreck."

Even that didn't bother me. Then he handed me his bill and I passed out.

Eating—America's Second Favorite Pastime

My PUBLISHER INSISTED that I write a chapter on diets, because she said diet books are all big sellers. Personally, I would rather have written this chapter about the other favorite pastime, which I know something about—which my sister Goldie knows even more about. But I'll get into that later. I mean, I'll write about it later.

So this chapter will be about diets, which I know very little about. I shouldn't have said that . . . which I know nothing about. But if it's going to make this book a big seller, I'm certainly not going to let my ignorance stand in the way.

Everyone in America is on a diet. Dieting has become a more popular sport than baseball, and it's played all year round. There are high-protein/low-fat diets; there are high-fat/low-protein diets; then there are low-carbohydrate/moderate-fat/high-protein diets; and high-carbohydrate/moderate-protein/

low-fat diets. And if that's not good enough for you, there are all-protein diets; all-carbohydrate diets; all-water diets; all-starvation diets; and even all-you-can-eat diets. That one's for fat people who want to stay fat.

Some diets are better than others, but you have to go to the right dinner parties and speak to the right overweight people to know which is which. There are diets named after the people who invented them, popularized them, used them, and died from them. One of the most popular diets is the Drinking Man's Diet. It's hard to know how many people use that one, because a lot of them don't know they're on it. (The nice thing about that joke is you can tell it five or six different ways and not get a laugh.)

Look, I'm not sure exactly how the Drinking Man's Diet works. Dean Martin's the authority on that one. Now, Dean has the reputation for being the biggest drinker in show business. I do a little drinking myself; I've had a few drinks with Dean. I've also had a few drinks with Phil Harris. But I'm not going to say which one drinks more, because if I did, the other one would never talk to me again. That is—if he remembers me.

This reminds me of a story. I've heard it before, but if I can listen to it again, so can you. Well, here it is. This is a story about Mr. & Mrs. Phillips. Her brother Joe had been living with them for seven years, and they were sick of him. So Mr. Phillips said, "Tonight at dinner I'll say the soup is hot, and you'll say it's cold. And if your brother agrees with me, you'll throw him out. And if he agrees with you, I'll throw him out." She said, "Good."

So at dinner they got into an argument about the soup. They said to Joe, "Is the soup hot or cold?"

And Joe said, "I'm not answering; I'm staying seven more years."

And that's how I feel about Dean Martin and Phil Harris. As far as I'm concerned they can both be the biggest drinkers.

You know, for a subject I know nothing about, I'm filling up a lot of pages.

Here's another thought for you. Everybody keeps talking about the overpopulation in our country. It's not an overpopulation problem, it's an overeating problem. If everyone in the country would lose ten pounds, we'd have enough room to build another state.

There are many theories why people overeat. Some experts say they do it because they have unhappy sex lives; that it's a form of substitution. But Elizabeth Taylor has a great appetite, so that theory is down the drain.

Personally, overeating was never a problem with me. As I told you, we were a family of seven sisters and five brothers, so there was no such thing as a—oh, by the way, we also had parents—anyway, when I was a kid, in our family there was no such thing as a diet. We didn't have enough food to cut down from. But my mother made the best gravy in the world. There was always a big pot of that marvelous gravy simmering on the stove. And whatever any of us brought home we'd throw into the pot: bread, bananas, garlic, onions, bread, string beans, fishheads, cheese, soup bones, turkey necks . . . and if we had a guest for dinner, my mother would add more bread. Those ingredients weren't bad, but it was the gravy that made it. Once my Uncle Frank was missing, and we even looked into the pot—everything went into that pot.

That's what we ate. I enjoyed it and that's all I knew. Later, when I was 14, I was doing an act with another fellow, called "Brown & Williams, Singers, Dancers and Rollerskaters." We were playing Albany, and I went into a restaurant and ordered my first full dinner. I had vegetable soup, a steak, lyonnaise potatoes, sliced tomatoes, apple pie, and coffee. I was sick for two days. I would have been sick longer, but I was booked.

In those days Brown and I were very rarely booked. Eating was a problem; for Brown, not for me. I had a little trick. I'd go into a restaurant, the waiter would come up, put a basket of bread on the table, and I'd say, "I'll order when my partner gets here." I'd eat all the bread, and then say, "I'm sorry, my partner didn't show up," and I'd leave.

The third time I went into this restaurant the waiter brought over an empty basket. I said, "Where's the bread?" and he said, "Your partner was here ahead of you."

I had another little trick. But I had to be careful not to do it more than once in the same restaurant. For instance, I'd go into Child's and sit next to a very well dressed man. I'd order pancakes, eggs, toast, and coffee. Then I'd say to the man, "Would you do me a favor? I'm trying to date the cashier, so when I pay my check I'll wave to you. And will you please wave back, because I want her to think I know nice people."

He'd say, "Sure," and when I got to the cashier, I'd say, "That gentleman is going to pay my check."

She'd say, "Who?", so I'd wave to the man. He'd wave back and I'd leave.

Just about the time I was running out of tricks, I fortunately met Gracie and didn't need them anymore. But all those years of doing bad acts and skipping meals left its mark. To this day my stomach still thinks I'm not doing well.

Actually, food is not important to me. For instance, steaks and chops—I don't touch them. Not that they can't be delicious, but you've got to cut them and chew them, and cut them and chew them, and chew them and cut them—if I have to work that hard, I want to get paid for eating.

Personally, I don't even like red meat. I like Red Buttons, I like Red Skelton, and I like Redd Foxx, but I don't like red meat. I like Steve Allen, but it doesn't fit here. I wish he'd change his name to Red Allen so I could give him a plug.

Well, you've waited long enough. Here it is: The George Burns Seven-Day Diet.

Monday

Breakfast
    4 prunes with low-fat milk
    2 cups coffee, black

Sometimes if I have a big weekend, I may only have three prunes. By the way, the milk goes over the prunes and also under them.

Lunch
    Bowl of soup
    1 slice French bread, toasted
    1 cup coffee, black

This is very flexible. If you haven't got French bread, rye bread is fine, or white bread, or rolls, or fruitcake. And it doesn't have to be a bowl of soup and a cup of coffee. It can be a bowl of coffee and a cup of soup. Whatever makes you happy. As I said, this is a very flexible diet.

Monday's breakfast.

Dinner
    Bowl of soup
    Mixed green salad
    Roast chicken
    Rice
    Green peas
    1 slice bread, buttered
    1 cup coffee, black
    Cookies

This is my big meal of the day. If I'm still hungry, I might include the one prune left over from breakfast. And the cookies must be very crisp so they make a noise in my mouth when I eat them. It sounds like applause, so I can eat and take bows at the same time.

Tuesday

Breakfast
> 1 small glass fresh orange juice
> Bowl bran cereal with milk
> 2 cups coffee, black

I let the cereal soak in the milk so it gets a little soggy. That way it doesn't make a noise when I'm eating, because I'm too tired from taking bows the night before.

Lunch
> Bowl of canned salmon with
>> white vinegar and lemon
> 1 English muffin, toasted
> 1 cup coffee, black

English muffins usually come sliced in half horizontally. I like each half sliced the same way, so the muffin is in four slices. That way I eat two slices and wind up eating just half a muffin. If it isn't sliced my way, I get very upset. I'm very temperamental about my muffins. I may stamp my foot or even go back to fruitcake.

Dinner
>Bowl of soup
>Mixed green salad
>Broiled fish
>Two vegetables
>1 slice bread, buttered
>1 cup coffee, black
>Ice cream

If it's white fish, then I have green vegetables. Green and white go together beautifully. But if the fish is red snapper, then I don't have green vegetables. I have yellow squash, even though I hate yellow squash. I can't stand a meal where the colors clash.

Wednesday

Breakfast
    1 small glass orange juice
    1 croissant with jelly
    1 cup coffee, black

My cook, Arlette, is a very attractive lady, and very nice. She always sees that my orange juice is freshly squeezed. And I see that she is. It gets the day off to a good start for both of us. I'm not a croissant fan, but I was always nuts about Maurice Chevalier, so I eat it in his memory.

Lunch
    2 soft-boiled eggs
    1 slice toast
    Pot of tea with lemon

I like eggs because they're so versatile. They can be poached, fried, scrambled, boiled—soft-boiled, hard-boiled, medium-boiled—shirred, and Benedicted. It's amazing how many things you can do with an egg after a chicken gets through with it.

Dinner
Shrimp cocktail
Mixed green salad
Carrots
1 potato, baked
Beef ribs
1 slice bread, buttered
1 cup coffee, black
Cookies

Remember, I told you I never touch red meat. That wasn't a lie, I don't touch the beef ribs. Arlette feeds them to me.

Thursday

Breakfast
> (Very light, nothing worth
> mentioning)

Lunch
> (Same as breakfast)

Dinner
This is my biggest meal of the week. I can't tell you
what it consists of, because I go out to dinner every
Thursday night. I go to the most expensive restaurant, and the reason I can't tell you what I eat is
because my host always orders for me. Look, I
couldn't be friends with Jack Benny for sixty years
and not have some of that rub off on me.

Breakfast
>   4 prunes with low-fat milk
>   2 cups coffee, black

There are other fruits I could eat for breakfast, but I prefer prunes because they've got more wrinkles than I have. I tried raisins once and they have good wrinkles, too. In fact, they have excellent wrinkles. But four raisins isn't much for breakfast, even for me. I wish they'd start making bananas with wrinkles; I'd like to try one of them.

Lunch
>   Bowl stove-hot alphabet soup
>   3 crackers, salted
>   3 crackers, unsalted
>   Pot of tea with lemon

In case you're wondering about the crackers, my doctor told me not to eat salt. But then again, I've got a nephew in the salt business. And the reason for the alphabet soup, I figure as long as I'm eating I might as well learn something.

Dinner
Whatever is in the doggie bag left over from that big dinner Thursday night.

Breakfast

    Spanish omelette
    French toast
    English muffin
    Irish coffee

This sounds like a ridiculous breakfast. Well, it is. But these are all our allies, and I don't want to offend anybody. Oh-oh, I left out Italy. Well, on my French toast I'll put a little Italian dressing.

Lunch

    Matzohs, eggs & onions
    1 iced tea

I must have matzohs, eggs, and onions at least once a week, because they remind me of Clayton, Jackson & Durante. And I loved Clayton, Jackson & Durante as much as I hate matzohs, eggs, and onions.

Dinner
This is my lightest meal of the week. It's the night I take out my host who took me out Thursday night.

Sunday

After eating all that food during the week, Sunday I eat nothing. I may have a martini or two . . . or three . . . but NO food . . . maybe four, I always like to end the week on a happy note . . . or five.

Author before Seven-Day Diet.   *Author after Seven-Day Diet.*

Sex Can Be Fun After 80, After 90, After 100, and After Lunch

BEFORE I START, let me get one thing straight; I'm not an authority on sex, I'm more of a fan. I think sex is nice; no family should be without it. Of course, there are other things that are just as important as sex, like uh . . . like uh . . . like . . . uh . . . well, I'll think of it later.

You're probably asking what has sex got to do with living to be over 100. I'm glad you asked that. As I said, I'm not an authority, but I've read a lot on the subject, I've also looked at a few pictures; and I understand sex relieves tension, anxiety, pressures, cures stuttering, removes pimples, prevents baldness, and has all sorts of benefits that a man of a hundred should be entitled to enjoy as much as a man of 90. Furthermore, nine out of ten doctors agree that sexual activity can lengthen your life. It can also shorten your life. I know one 40-year-old fellow who was very active sexually with this lady, until her husband shot him.

One of my closest friends, George Jessel, was quite a guy with the ladies. Those medals he wore weren't all for good conduct. His many escapades didn't shorten his life, but they led to some pretty harrowing experiences. I'll tell you about just one incident:

There was Millie, this beautiful showgirl who worked in "Shubert's Gaities of 1919." She was in love with Georgie and Georgie was crazy about her. The only trouble was she was very jealous of him, and every time she'd catch him in bed with another girl, she'd hit him over the head with a vase, a telephone, an ashtray . . . anything she could lift. Jessel didn't like that; it was giving him headaches. So he hired a young fellow named Leo Davis to live with him. Leo's job was whenever there was a knock on the door, he would jump in bed with the girl, and Jessel would answer the door, because Georgie was afraid of Millie.

Well, one day it happened. There was a knock on the door, Leo jumped in bed with the girl, and Jessel answered the door. When he came back, he said, "Thank God it wasn't Millie, it was a telegram."

Millie said, "How could it be me? I'm in bed here with Leo." You'd think this would stop Jessel's

Author researching this chapter.

headaches, but it didn't. By the time they split up he was two inches shorter.

These days sex is much more out in the open than it used to be, especially among the younger generation. There's nothing they won't talk about; no words are off limits. And they say them out loud, they write them on walls, they even put them on T-shirts. In my day, if I said a dirty word, my mother would wash my mouth out with soap. I had bubbles coming out of my ears five days a week.

But with me it was all talk. When I was young my thing was show business. The only kind of girl I was interested in was a girl I could work with, a girl who could get laughs, because I was a straight man. You know what a straight man is. He just repeats everything. The comedian says something, he repeats it and waits for the comedian to get the laugh.

Well, I met this pretty girl; her name was Lily Delight, and I said to her, "How about you and me doing something together?"

She said, "Sure," and invited me up to her apartment, locked the door, turned the lights down low, and said, "How would you like to have a drink?" So I repeated, "How would you like to have a drink?" And she had one. Then she said, "Would you like to have another one?" And I repeated, "Would you like to have another one?"

After the fourth drink she said, "How about

going into the bedroom?" So I repeated, "How about going into the bedroom?" Then she said, "How about turning out the lights?" So I said, "How about turning out the lights?" She turned out the lights and I went home . . . she wasn't getting any laughs, so I left.

Even with Gracie, for me the laughs came first. We had a marvelous marriage, and not because I was a great lover. I never remember kissing Gracie and getting applause. When Gracie and I went to bed, I'd sing her two or three songs until she fell asleep. I found out after you've been married for twenty years it's much easier to sing.

Look, I don't want you to think from all this that I'm knocking sex. It's still better than sliced tomatoes with the skins on.

My career is very important to me right now; it always has been. But I try to balance it out with a little fun. I entertain at home, I go out to parties, I go to nice restaurants, and I make it a point to squeeze in a little female companionship. I try not to squeeze too hard; I don't want to break the skin on the tomatoes. I don't know what that means, but it sounds exciting.

When I made my last movie, I was being examined for insurance, and the doctor asked me how old I was. I told him 86, and he said, "When did sex stop for you?"

I said, "At three o'clock this morning." You're right—I passed the exam.

Some people think that sex isn't for older people, that they should taper off, or that they should stop altogether. That's silly. Age isn't the problem; the problem is getting a girl. And if you can't get one 22, get one 25.

I'm very honest about my life, off-stage and on. And even when I'm lying I tell people I'm lying . . . which is not true. I get a lot of mail, and people are always asking me how I can do what I do at my age. In fact, I just got a letter this morning from a man who said exactly that: "George, how can you do what you do at your age?" So I answered, "I wear gloves." A good question deserves a good answer.

Here's another letter:

Dear George,
    I'm a year older than you are, and I just married a girl 22. My problem is I'm afraid I won't be able to satisfy her. I would appreciate any suggestions.

I wrote back and said, "Take in a boarder." Three months later he called on the phone and told me my advice worked; his wife was pregnant. I said, "What about the boarder?" and he said, "She's pregnant, too."

Here's another letter:

Dear George,
    I'm getting along in years and I'm having a problem with my sex life. A friend of mine who's two years older than I am says he has sex three times a week.

So I wrote back and said, "If he can say it, you can say it." I thought that was a pretty good answer. You know, when it comes to this subject, you can't always believe what people say, including me.

Here's one that hits home from a fellow named Frank in Altoona:

Dear George,
    Every time my wife and I go to bed as soon as I try to touch her she says, "Please, I've got a headache." What should I do?

My answer was, "After dinner, when you and your wife are watching television, offer her two aspirin. She'll say she hasn't got a headache, and you've got her. The next night you're on your own."

Here's one from a young lady:

Dear George,
    I've been reading a lot of your publicity, and is it really true that at your age you still have an active sex life?

I wrote back, "I don't think I can make the Olympic Sex Team, but I can certainly be sitting on the bench if they need me." That was kind of a snippy answer, but her letter annoyed me. I was really upset with her; she didn't include her telephone number.

Here's one I don't believe:

Dear George,
    I've been married for 8 years. I love my wife very much, but she's a nymphomaniac. What should I do?

I said, "Stop writing letters and count your blessings."

Here's one that just came in this morning:

Dear George,
    Please stay out of my business!
Dear Abby

Well, that takes care of the letters. But I can't close this chapter without leaving you with a few serious thoughts. You shouldn't be too casual about sex; you've got to try to make it exciting. After couples are married for a while they tend to take sex for granted. They don't even bother to lock the door. Big mistake. Sex has to be behind locked doors. If what you're doing can be done out in the open, you might as well be pitching horseshoes.

I know a couple who always left the door open when they were making love. One night in the middle of everything their little girl walked in. The mother raised her head and said, "Elsie, go out and close the door . . . I'll be with you in a second." That took care of little Elsie, and it also took care of the husband.

And here's another thought. Very important. No matter how old you are, remember that sex is a special part of your life and should not be neglected. The key word is moderation. Beware of doing it so often that you haven't enough energy left to finish what you set out to accomplish.

Relatives Can Be Nice—
If They're Not Yours

IF YOU WERE paying attention, you'll remember I said that sex was nice and no family should be without it. This also applies to children. Children are wonderful. They say cute things you can repeat at parties. They hug you and kiss you and muss your hair. They jump in bed with you at all hours of the night. They laugh when you make funny faces at them. When things get dull they're always there to play horsie with you. And when they're growing up, they make you proud and happy and give your marriage not only a purpose but also a sense of fulfillment. That last phrase sounds so good it belongs in a sermon. Come to think of it, that's where I heard it. If Milton Berle can steal from me, I can certainly steal from Billy Graham.

Anyway, children can be great. They've also been known to take a few years off your life, like fifty or sixty. Since I've made it to 87 so far, obviously my two kids and my seven grandchildren haven't been too hard on me. On the other hand, the fact that I have an unlisted phone number and move a lot might have something to do with it.

I knew a couple who were constantly worrying about their son. If Little Billy was away for the day and didn't come back on time, the parents were walking the floor and calling the Missing Persons Bureau. If it was chilly and he went out without his sweater, they couldn't eat their dinner. If it was sunny, they'd drive miles to bring Little Billy his hat. And if it started to rain, that was two or three years off their lives right there. Now, all this concern may not seem so strange to you—and it wouldn't to me, either—but I happen to know that Little Billy is going to be 61 in January.

It's not always the children's fault; some parents just won't let go. You know people like that. You may be one of them. You worry if the kid studies all the time and has no friends. And if he has friends and doesn't study, that's no good, either. You worry if your teenage daughter doesn't have dates, and if she has a lot of dates, you worry about what she's doing to be so popular. You're upset that your daughter is too young to get married, and a year later when she's still not married you're upset that you've got an old maid on your hands. Your son's married to a girl who doesn't believe in working, and you're sick about it. And you're incensed because your daughter's no-good husband wants her to work.

Birds don't have these problems. As soon as the baby birds learn to fly, they leave the nest. It's bye-bye, birdie. Mama and papa bird never see them again, unless they meet across a crowded birdbath. They've got the right idea. I've never met a worried bird. On the other hand, I've never met a 100-year-old bird. I've got a parrot who says he's 64, but he lies a lot. (If I can steal from Billy Graham, the parrot can steal from me.)

Like most parents today, I always wanted my children to have everything I had when I was a kid. In my case, that was no problem—I had nothing. When you have seven sisters and four brothers, one thing you don't suffer from is too much attention. I can't remember my parents ever screaming or hollering at me. They couldn't; they didn't know my name. For five years I was "Hey, you!" And after that my father kept getting me mixed up with my brother Sammy. That made me feel bad, but my brother Willy felt worse. My father kept getting him mixed up with my sister Sarah. Why, I don't know. Her feet were twice as big as his.

These days a college education costs anywhere from twenty to forty thousand dollars. And that doesn't include the postage for the kid to write home for more money every week. Yet every parent thinks a college education for their kids is a must, even if it means mortgaging the house, working their fingers to the bone, and winding up spending a week at Cedars-Sinai—which is the only thing more expensive than four years at college.

It wasn't that way with me. When I finished fourth grade, my father said, "Congratulations, Sammy, from now on you're on your own." That was the end of my schooling. I brought back all the chalk I'd stolen from my teacher, Miss Hollander, and she gave me my ring back.

When my son, Ronnie, was about 17 he was a tall, good-looking kid, outgoing and with a good sense of humor. One day Gracie said, "George . . . Ozzie and Harriet have their two sons on their show, why don't we put Ronnie in show business?"

I said, "That's a good idea. I'll call up Ozzie and Harriet and ask them if they could use another son." After I didn't get my laugh, I said, "Gracie, that is a good idea. We'll put Ronnie in show business." Unfortunately, we neglected to discuss it with Ronnie.

I started him with just a few lines on our show. He did well, so I made the part bigger and bigger. The audience loved him, and he was on the show for years. But he was never really interested. He was more interested in the girls who used to hang out at the Luau restaurant. That's the career Ronnie was interested in.

After he'd been with us a few years I thought Ronnie had a chance to be a very good actor. So one day I told him that I wanted him to go to New York and study at the Lee Strasberg Actors Studio. I reminded him that Strasberg had turned out some of America's greatest actors, and if he studied there for two years, he might turn out to be one of the greats. He said, "Thanks, dad, but I'm not leaving the Luau for that."

I said, "Ronnie, I know the girls at the Luau are very pretty, but there are girls in New York who are just as pretty. And they've got the same things that the girls at the Luau have, and in the exact same place." I couldn't convince him, and Ronnie went on to become one of the greats at the Luau.

Actually, Ronnie has done fine and is very happy now. But at that time it really upset me; it took a couple of years off my life. If it weren't for that, today I'd be 89. But it did teach me an important lesson: you mustn't try to run your children's lives. My father made the same mistake with me. When I wanted to go into show business, my father was shocked. He said, "Show business! What kind of business is that? There's no future in it! You'll be nothing like that Al Jolson kid you're running around with! Get into something substantial—make felt hats for a living!" For years I kept hearing "Make felt hats! Make felt hats!" I'm not sure, but I think I made the right decision. But to this day I feel so guilty that whenever I take a shower I wear a felt hat.

Trying to run your children's lives is bad enough, but it's even worse when you get older and they try to run yours. They tell you what to eat, how to dress, what time to get up, what time to go to bed; they won't let you drive your car, they help you when you sit, they help you when you stand up, they help you into senility. The older you get the more they treat you like a baby. You don't know whether to walk with a cane or put a nipple in your mouth. And watch it when they tell you you're not capable of handling your money. They'll do it for you. That could be the last time you see your money and the last you see of your kids.

Like my Uncle Frank. His kids took all his money, every cent he had, and they invested it in some little electronics business that some friend had started in his garage. I said, "Frank, how could you let them do this?" He said, "They're my kids and they want to help me." Anyway, this little company turned out to be a smash, and Uncle Frank is worth millions of dollars. (Wait a minute—why did I tell you this story? It contradicts my whole premise. Okay, so I made a mistake. What do you expect from a writer who should be making felt hats?)

Children aren't the only ones who can shorten your life. The rest of your relatives are doing their share, too. That includes sisters, brothers, aunts, uncles, nephews, nieces, cousins, grandparents, in-laws, and some house pets. Every single one of them has the capacity to keep you from reaching 100.

When you're born you start out life with two things: diaper rash and relatives. Both can be very annoying, but you can get rid of the rash. And if you happen to be doing well, your relatives love you, they're all over the place, they can't do enough for you. But if you're not doing well, you couldn't find a relative if you looked in the Yellow Pages. It almost makes failure worthwhile.

There's nothing worse than the relative who comes for a fun visit and is still there five years later. The first two years aren't too bad; you only have a couple of nervous breakdowns. But after that it's murder. They have dinner with you every night; at breakfast they beat you to the morning paper; they have their favorite chair that you'd better not sit in; they don't like your friends so they bring in their own; when you watch television they're right there to change the channel—and after five years you're so confused you say to your wife, "We've lived with him long enough, let's pack and go home."

Getting back to my family again, there was no such thing as relatives moving in. We didn't have

A few of the author's relatives.

(© Dave Repp–DPI)

room for them. We didn't have room for us. And if any of us left home, there was no coming back. I'll never forget when my sister Teresa was married to Charlie Kalendar. They had a big fight and she showed up at the house one day. She said, "Mama, I'm teaching Charlie a lesson. I'm moving in with you." My mother said, "If you really want to teach him a lesson, you go home and I'll move in with you." My mother was something. She was ready for any emergency.

How about that thing that happened in Akron, Ohio. Jascha Heifetz, one of the world's greatest violinists, was giving a concert there. And that night there was a terrible storm, thunder and lightning, and very few people showed up. So the manager walked out on the stage and said that he was sorry, but Mr. Heifetz wouldn't appear that night and they were refunding everybody's money. Well, this one fellow went backstage and said, "Mr. Heifetz, I'm one of your biggest fans. My wife and I drove all the way from Youngstown to hear you. At least sing one song for us."

That has nothing to do with the subject, but it's an amusing story, and I thought it would be nice to end the chapter with a laugh. Wait a minute—I can't end the chapter here. I just realized that I talked about my son, Ronnie, and never mentioned my daughter, Sandra. She'll never forgive me. I better mention her. In fact, I'll mention her four times—Sandra, Sandra, Sandra, Sandra.

If It Wears Out,
You Can Get a New One

THERE'S NO POINT in kidding yourself—when you get older you just naturally slow up. Your body doesn't work as well; you wear out a little. I'm waiting for this to happen to me. And when it does I'll make the best of it. Right now I'm 87, and there isn't a thing I can't do now that I couldn't do when I was 18. I can do more now than when I was 18 . . . I did nothing when I was 18 . . . I was pathetic when I was 18 . . . I was even worse when I was 17 . . . I wasn't so hot when I was 25, either. I saved everything for now. I hate to brag, but I'm very good at now.

But I've got to admit, lately I've noticed a few signs of slowing down. For instance, my cuticles are not what they used to be. And when I'm smoking a cigar and blow the smoke out, I notice that the rings are smaller, and they're not as round as they used to be. And when I drink a martini, instead of two I'm only using one olive. The truth is the truth: I'm not what I used to be. If I keep going downhill like this, I'll feel like I did when I was 18 . . . when I was pathetic . . . when I did nothing— Wait a minute, I'm repeating myself, I just said that. See how fast I'm going downhill.

Everybody begins to wear out at a different age. I've got this friend, my age, who's always been a bachelor and a big ladies' man. I ran into him the other day, and said, "Charlie, how're you doing?"

He said, "George, you'll never believe it, I'm not what I used to be. I still go to the park every morning and sit on that same bench, but what happens? I see a beautiful girl jog by, and my brain tells me to run over and see if she'll share some Gatorade with me. But by the time I'm able to lift myself off the bench, she's home, taken a shower, and had breakfast."

"Charlie," I said, "that's a very depressing story."

He said, "You don't know the half of it. I've got a refrigerator full of Gatorade."

But I'll tell you something. Charlie's lucky, I'm lucky, all us older folks are lucky. Science is on our side. When things wear out, now they've got spare parts for them. In the old days you were stuck with what you had. There was very little they could do for you. True, George Washington had wooden teeth, but that didn't work out too well for him. Every time Martha saw one of her ladyfriends taking splinters out of her lips, George was in trouble.

Then there was Captain Hook. He lost his hand, and they made him an artificial hand out of a hook. He could pick up things, but every time he scratched himself he couldn't sit down for four days. And there was Long John Silver with his wooden leg. He lost a Charleston contest on account of that.

Today it's different. You can get an artificial heart, an artificial kidney, a metal hip socket, a metal elbow joint, a metal kneecap. . . . Today you don't have to worry about getting old, you have to worry about rusting. You don't need a family doctor, just a mechanic who makes house calls. It's great. Every once in a while you have a lube, oil, and tune-up, and instead of an annual physical you get a 10,000-mile checkup. By the time I get to be 100, people won't be dying anymore. They'll be traded in. And if you can't work out a trade, you can always leave your body to the Auto Club.

All this isn't as far-fetched as it sounds. They already have eye banks. And pretty soon they'll have stores where you can pick out whatever you need. When you're out shopping for a pair of shoes, you can stop off and pick up a kidney or two. If it's a reliable store, they'll give you a ten-day free trial.

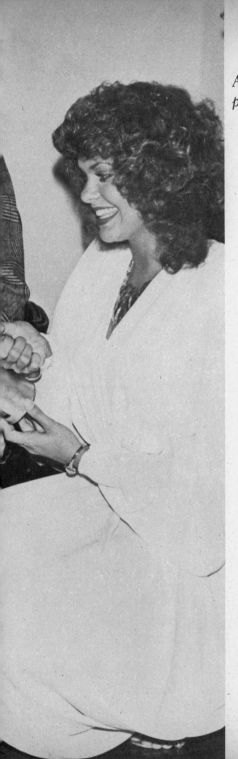

Author having his spare
parts tuned up.

And if it doesn't work out, you return the kidneys. There's a certain item I'd like to try out for ten days, but so far there's no such store.

I've got great faith in the American free enterprise system. I can see the day when you not only can get all these parts, but you'll be able to get them in different colors. A customer will walk in and say, "I'd like a blue kidney and an orange liver. Those are my school colors. And while you're at it, throw in a couple of those in black for evening wear."

It would be awful if you were new on the inside and old on the outside. Plastic surgery has taken care of that. You can't be sure of anyone's age today. They fix your nose, they adjust your ears, they remove extra chins, they de-puff your eyes, they alter your breasts—they can make them smaller or they can make them bigger—they can even remold your rear end. I went out the other night with an attractive girl who told me she was 20. Later I found out I was dancing with a 70-year-old man. I'm not well. I should have guessed when she told me her name was Irving.

It's amazing what people will go through to change their appearance. I'm going back a few years—a friend of mine named Jimmy Davidson was going around with this very pretty girl. He was crazy about her and wanted to marry her. She liked him, too, but she was taller than he was. She said,

"Jimmy, I love you, and if you were two inches taller, I'd marry you." So Jimmy put a stretching machine in his basement, and every day for three months he went down there and stretched himself. And if Jimmy had lived, he would have made her a very good husband. Nice fellow. It's a shame he died a quarter of an inch short.

In show business (which, by the way, I'm in when I'm not dabbling in the literary world) appearances are very important. To a beautiful leading lady or a handsome leading man, looks can be crucial to their careers. The minute that skin starts to sag, they run to the nearest plastic surgeon. Then they sneak out of town to New Haven to break in their new face. If they like the way it looks, they bring it back to Hollywood.

It isn't just for romantic leads, it also goes for singers, dancers, and comedians. Look at my friend Phyllis Diller. It's no secret, she talks about it on the stage, but she's had her face lifted so many times she can do it herself now.

Some performers are sensitive about their most distinctive features. One day at my club Kirk Douglas said, "George, now that I'm getting a little older, do you think I ought to take the dimple out of my chin?" I said, "Kirk, don't touch it. It's a nice place to keep salt." So he left it alone and he's still doing great. Of course, talent has something to do with it, too. My brother Sammy in Orange, New Jersey, has three dimples and two chins and can't get a job.

There are other performers who would be out of their minds to change certain features. Those features are their trademark. When Jimmy Durante started in show business he was worried about that big nose of his. He thought it might hinder his career. He went to three plastic surgeons and got estimates. But they were so expensive he had to play little cafés to get enough money to have it fixed. Before he knew it, his nose was such a big hit that he forgot about the operation. And he and his nose stayed together for the rest of his life.

Can you imagine Bob Hope or Danny Thomas with a normal profile? They'd have to fire their nose writers. Fanny Brice didn't exactly have a small nose, either. She kept it that way so Barbra Streisand could play her life in the movie. Where would Maurice Chevalier have been if some plastic surgeon had pulled back his protruding lower lip? Every time he sang "Louise" the breeze would have blown his socks off. Eddie Cantor—would he have been such a success without those big banjo eyes? And can you imagine Dolly Parton without that big head of hair?

I don't say appearance isn't important, but what's all the fuss about? Tall, dark, and handsome isn't the answer. Look at Mickey Rooney. He's

short, bald, and dumpy, and he's had eight wives
. . . and who knows what happened in between.

To me what is really important are the miracles
they're performing today with the major organs in
our bodies. There are thousands of people alive today because of the heart-bypass operation alone. I'm
one of them. That's for the arteries leading to the
heart. For the heart itself, there's the pacemaker, the
heart transplant, and new valves. They're even
working on an artificial heart. If they perfect that, I
might be around forever. Why am I talking about
only living to be 100 or more? I'm not going to die; I
won't be able to. The only thing is, with all those
spare parts I may wind up being somebody else.
Whoever he is, I hope he stays in show business.
I've got a few songs I haven't used yet. Maybe even a
funny line or two.

As I'm writing this, thousands and thousands of working men and women are about to retire. I've got one word for them—don't! I hate to tell thousands and thousands of people what to do, but I feel very strongly about this. In fact, I feel so strongly that for the rest of this chapter I'm not going to be funny. No jokes. Well, maybe one or two. No! . . . when I feel strongly about a subject I don't fool around. Look, it's not easy not to be funny. I'm a natural humorist. And that's better than being an unnatural humorist. So it's going to be difficult writing this chapter without a few laughs. I hope I don't hurt myself. But if I do, it's worth it for a subject I feel so strongly about. By the way, what is the subject? Oh yeah . . . retirement.

Okay, let's say you are one of those who retires at 65. You stumble home from your farewell party at the office, your eyes still moist from all the praise heaped on you, and your back raw from all the times they've slapped it. Poor devils. They'll soon find out how tough it is to get along without you. But that's their problem. You don't have to worry about them anymore. You don't have to worry about anyone. The pressure is off. You're retired. From now on you can do what you want to do, and you've got all day to do it in. (I could have made that last line funny, but I'm holding back.)

The first week is fine. A nice mixture of work and play. Why not? There are all those chores you've been putting off for months. You fix the broken stereo, paint a wall or two, catch up on your correspondence, redo the petunia bed . . . you even get in a round of golf and a little fishing off the pier. The time whips by. You're happy. Your wife is happy. You bump into one of your buddies from work and you note the harassed look on his face. Boy, would you hate to be him! This is what life is all about. The greatest. No wonder they call it the Golden Years.

That's the first week. Now it's 9:00 A.M., the start of your second week. You've already been up for two hours, had three cups of coffee, read the paper from end to end, including every classified ad. Hey, how about making a nice breakfast for the little woman? Good idea. You'll bring her breakfast in bed. First off, she's mad at you for waking her. And it turns out she doesn't want breakfast in bed; she hates breakfast in bed. And why are you doing this for her? You must feel guilty. Is something going on between you and that divorcée you keep seeing in the apartment house laundry room? She says, "That's the last time you'll ever wash our clothes!" It's a whole big thing. But at least you've used up an hour to calm her down.

So now it's ten o'clock. You say to her, "We've got the whole day to ourselves, sweetheart. What'll we do?" She says, "I don't know about you, but I'm playing bridge."

That takes care of her. So now what do you do? Clean out your closet? You did that last week. You can't water the petunias again because it's raining. Your desk? Hey, great, it's a mess. That should kill a couple of hours.

Okay, so the day's going a little slowly; you'll have lunch with some of the gang at work. They're probably dying to see you. And sure enough, when you call them that's what they tell you. They also tell you they have appointments and you'll have to try them again sometime. But it's not a total loss. You ask the office manager who filled your vacancy and he tells you that you didn't leave any. (That's funny, but I didn't say that, the office manager did. He must be a natural humorist, too.)

Somehow you manage to get through the day. The movie helps. It's the first time you ever went to a movie in the afternoon. And you're not alone, either. There are three others in the theater. Don't get discouraged, every day won't be like this. There will be days that are worse. In fact, if you live to be 100, you've got thirty-five years of this to look forward to.

I know that for some people retirement works out fine. They adjust to it. I don't know how they do it, but they enjoy it. I also know that for a great many others it presents lots of problems.

One problem is that all those things you thought were so much fun when you were working are not so much fun when you're retired. Take the golf nut who couldn't wait to get away from his desk to squeeze in nine holes. Now he can play every day. And not just nine holes. He can play eighteen, or thirty-six, or thirty-seven, if he can still walk. After a month of this he hates golf and he can't stand grass. So he figures he'll try fishing. He buys himself a fly rod, hip boots, and all the paraphernalia, including the fishing hat with a full assortment of colored flies stuck all around it, and a big button right in front that reads "Keep America Green." Now he's ready to go fishing. I really didn't have to say that; he could hardly play golf in that outfit.

He finds himself a beautiful stream, and after a month of standing up to his ass in water, he can't look at another fish. But that's perfectly okay, because the fish can't look at him, either. So he decides to stay home for a while. After three weeks of looking at his wife, he's back fishing again.

Then again, retiring constitutes a very big change in your life. And like any abrupt change it can be a shock to your system. Think how difficult it would be for Sylvester Stallone to stop making "Rocky" movies; or for Burt Reynolds to become a monk; or for Bob Hope to let someone else do the commercials on his show. I could give you more illustrations like this, but I'm restraining myself because I feel very strongly about this chapter.

To me the biggest danger of retirement is what it can do to your attitude. When you have all that time on your hands, you think old, you act old. It's a mistake. I see people who, the minute they get to be 65, start rehearsing to be old. They start taking little steps, they practice grunting when they sit down and grunting when they get up, they drop food on themselves, they take little naps when you're talking to them, and by the time they get to be 70 they've made it—they're a hit—they're now old! Not me. When I was 65 I won a Charleston contest. I know it's hard to believe, but you can look it up. Lionel

Author trying to persuade young lady to retire.

Barrymore came in second. I don't know how I remembered that. Sometimes my memory amazes me.

Attitude is all-important. When you're around my age you've got to keep occupied. You've got to do something that will get you out of bed. I never made a nickel in bed. Yeah, get out of bed. Find something that will make you do it—like an interest . . . a hobby . . . a business . . . a pretty girl—there we are back in bed again. I hope that didn't shock you. I do a lot of talking. At my age at least let me talk about it.

I can truthfully say that the idea of retiring has never entered my mind. My retiring might have entered other people's minds, but not mine. When I first started in vaudeville I was strictly small-time. I'd be lying if I said I did the worst act in the world; I wasn't that good. At many a performance at the finish of my act the audience would get to their feet and holler, "Retire! Retire!" And some of them didn't put it that delicately. I'll never forget when I was 21 I was living with a fellow named Mike Marks, and one morning when we were having breakfast a rock came through the window with a note tied to it. It read, "Retire," and Mike Marks did. I never told him the note was for me.

Years later, when Gracie retired in '58, I could have retired, too. I could have taken it easy, gone fishing in my hip boots, or played golf in them—but I didn't. And even today I don't have to do what I'm doing. I could give up the whole thing. I don't have to travel around giving concerts to thousands of people, making movies, doing television specials, recording country albums, being a sex symbol, taking out all those young girls—I don't have to put up with all that nonsense. I don't even have to write this book; I could be reading it. Let that funny office manager who said, "You didn't leave a vacancy" write it.

I've got a manager, Irving Fein, who's in his 60s. He's got me booked for the next five years, and if I even mention retirement, he starts to cry. He's very emotional. I once canceled a Wednesday night concert and Irving cried for two hours. I never realized he was that interested in my welfare. I can't quit. It would break the kid's heart. So you see, I have to keep working until Irving is old enough to retire.

One of the greatest tragedies of retirement is the waste of talent it can represent. Some of our most impressive accomplishments came from people who were over 65 . . . over 75 . . . over 80.

George Bernard Shaw was still writing plays at 93.

At 89 Albert Schweitzer was running a hospital in Africa.

Alexander Graham Bell was still inventing things at 74. In 1875 he invented the telephone. I happen to know it's true, because his first words were, "Can you hear me, George?" He would have invented the telephone sooner, but the line was busy.

At 91 Eamon de Valera served as President of Ireland.

At 88 Konrad Adenauer was Chancellor of Germany.

Michelangelo, who painted the ceiling of the Sistine Chapel, one of the artistic wonders of the world, was still painting at 88. Hey, 88! I'm gonna be 88 next year, I think I'll try a few ceilings. Who knows, if I'm good at it, maybe Rabbi Magnin will let me do his temple.

What about Pablo Picasso? He was still working at 92. Picasso was one of our all-time great nude painters. And he wasn't bad with his clothes on, either.

Actually, I never understood Picasso's work. I'm more of a Grandma Moses fan. She was still painting at 100. Now, you're expecting me to say that I carried her books home from school or something like that. I couldn't say that; I never knew Grandma Moses. I knew the original Moses, the one of the Ten Commandments fame.

Probably the most famous inventor of all times

was Thomas Edison. He gave us the electric light, the phonograph, and talking pictures. Then, at 84, he invented the dictaphone and the duplicating machine. In fact, he accomplished so much that when they depicted his life on the screen they had to use two actors to play him—Mickey Rooney and Spencer Tracy. What a man that Edison was—over 1,100 inventions! Next year instead of painting ceilings maybe I'll invent a few things.

At 81 Benjamin Franklin helped write the United States Constitution. He must have gotten smarter later in life, because at 46 he was still playing with kites.

Adolph Zukor at 91 was still Chairman of the Board of Paramount Pictures. Mr. Zukor and I were very close friends. Gracie and I made about a dozen pictures for him. I used to go into his office and play gin rummy with him. We were playing once, and he knocked and said, "I'm going down with ten." But he had eleven . . . he had a seven and four.

I said, "Before we throw the cards in, Mr. Zukor, you know, Gracie and I are now doing this picture with Bing Crosby, and in it Crosby sings five songs. How about letting me sing one of those songs?"

He looked right at me and said, "George, Bing Crosby, one of our major stars, is going to sing all five songs."

So I looked back at him and said, "Mr. Zukor, you got eleven."

He said, "George, you and Gracie have been with us now for six years. Do you like working for Paramount?"

"I love it."

"Do you like living out here?"

"I love it."

"You wouldn't want to move back east?"

"No, sir."

Then he said, "How much is seven and four?"

I said, "Ten."

Bing Crosby sang the five songs, Gracie and I never moved back east, and I never won a game of gin rummy from Mr. Zukor.

At 89 Mary Baker Eddy was directing the Christian Science Church.

At 85 Coco Chanel was the head of her fashion-design firm.

And Trixie Hicks is still at it at 82.

W. Somerset Maugham wrote *Points of View* at 84.

Leo Tolstoy wrote *I Cannot Be Silent* at 82.

Winston Churchill wrote *A History of the English-Speaking Peoples* at 82.

George Burns wrote *Living It Up* at 80, and at 84 he wrote *The Third Time Around*, and now at 87 he's writing *How to Live to Be 100—Or More*. I figure if I can plug those other writers, why shouldn't I do it for myself?

I could go on for pages telling you about people who did remarkable things late in life. But let me point out one thing. The man with the toughest job in the world is over 70—The President of the United States, Ronald Reagan.

But as for myself, I've said this before and I don't mind saying it again: I—will—never—retire! I firmly believe that you should keep working as long as you can. And if you can't, try to find something that will interest you. Don't wait for it to happen; make it happen. Keep your mind and body active.

Remember, you can't help getting older, but you don't have to get old.

Open Your Wallet and Say Ahhhh!

IF YOU'RE GOING TO LIVE to be 100 or more, sooner or later you'll be dealing with one of the oldest professions on earth—the doctor, or the healer. Of course, it's not *the* oldest. *The* oldest profession involves providing a different kind of service to the public. You don't go to school for it, and you don't go into practice afterward. In fact, if you're still practicing, you can't be one.

But enough of that talk; it's disgusting. Let's talk about the profession dedicated to keeping you out of bed. The medical profession these days is a very honorable one, and also very lucrative. There's a good reason why mothers want their daughters to marry doctors. They do very well. Their yearly income is right up there with basketball players, and they can be half their size. Not only that, they don't have to pay doctors' bills.

When I was a kid, our neighborhood doctor was a little old man with a black bag and a three-piece, pin-stripe suit. He had a little old office downstairs in his little old house. He had an ugly old nurse, and he made house calls, probably to get away from her. One day he got a young pretty nurse and the old ugly one disappeared, and so did the house calls.

I'll never forget old Dr. Stern. When one of us got sick, my mother would call him on her direct line; she'd open the window and shout down the street. If the doctor was out, he had an answering service . . . Mrs. Goldberg. She had the candy store next to his house, and she would shout back, "Call later! He's out!"

My mother had a little trick to hold down Dr. Stern's fees. Don't forget, in those days a house call cost $2.00. She'd lump the symptoms of all twelve of us kids together, and then she would tell the doctor that my brother Sammy had all those ailments. So that way the doctor thought he was treating only one patient.

Once Dr. Stern left the house, my mother would distribute the right medicine to the right kid for the right ailment. This system worked perfectly for about twelve years. Then my sisters became teenagers and started having different sorts of medical problems. When we gave Sammy the same symptoms, the doctor began to worry. Sammy didn't know. He just couldn't understand why none of the girls in the neighborhood would go out with him. My mother finally told him on his 28th birthday. So Sammy came to me and asked me to straighten out all the girls in the neighborhood. And I did. They still wouldn't go out with him.

Incidentally, they say things like this don't happen, but Dr. Stern at 81 married that beautiful 24-year-old nurse. They would have been very happy together if he hadn't died on their honeymoon.

That neighborhood of ours was so poor the only ailment anyone could afford was a fever. You starved that. We couldn't afford a cold because you had to feed it. There were no health plans in those days, and even $2.00 for a house call was rough. But Dr. Stern was very considerate. He gave Mr. Klein six months to live, and when he found out he couldn't pay his bill, he gave him another six months. By the way, Mr. Klein outlived Dr. Stern and married that pretty young nurse. It broke my brother Sammy's heart because she was the only one who went out with him. My neighborhood was poor, but very active.

You're not going to believe this, but in those days people didn't go to a hospital. You had to pay as much as six or eight dollars for a private room. By the time you had X rays and medication, your bill could run up to sixteen or seventeen dollars. You could go to Europe for that.

And if you went to a hospital, you were taking a big gamble. The sign out front read, ENTER AT YOUR OWN RISK. That's not quite true, but neither is that stuff about my brother Sammy. But if I can lie about my own family, I can certainly lie about a hospital sign.

We kids never saw the inside of a hospital. If any of us got sick, my mother would bring out the chicken soup. Believe me, it was cheaper than medicine and tasted a lot better. Of course, it didn't work for broken bones. For broken bones she gave us boiled beef. Once our next-door neighbor got sick and my mother gave her chicken soup. But she asked for a second opinion, so my mother gave her vegetable soup.

Medicine is different today. Every doctor's a specialist. Each one has his own disease. There are so many young doctors who can't even get into practice until a new disease opens up. They're backed up clear to herpes.

Nowadays you go to your doctor, he looks you over and sends you to a specialist. So you go to the specialist, he looks you over and sends you to another specialist. You go to him, and he doesn't even bother to look you over; his specialty is sending people to specialists. He hasn't even got a name on his door, just an arrow. Look, I'm not knocking specialists—those kids have to make a living, too. It gets expensive putting gas in your three Jaguars. It's not their fault that the doctor who knows everything about the ear gets more for a visit than the doctor who knows everything about the entire body. The more I think about it, the more I'm in favor of specialists. I don't want to go to a doctor with a sprained ankle and have my tonsils taken out. And if I die on an operating table, I want the satisfaction of knowing that the right guy was responsible.

Wednesday is the international day of the week when doctors all over the world close up shop and play golf. So please don't get sick on Wednesday unless you plan to collapse on a golf course. If you feel like getting sick, make it Monday or Tuesday. Forget Thursday, because your doctor might be getting over the bad game of golf he played on Wednesday. Friday's a little shaky because he's getting ready for his big weekend. Come to think of it, Monday is out, too. He's recovering from his weekend. So there's only one thing to do—get sick on Tuesday—between ten and five. Tuesday night is a big theater night for doctors.

Actually, I know a lot of doctors, and I'm very fond of them. They're a very dedicated group. One of the most dedicated isn't really a doctor at all, he's my friend Danny Kaye. Not many people know this, but Danny always wanted to be a doctor. When he was just a kid he told his parents when he grew up he'd like to go to medical school and become a famous surgeon. It got such a laugh he decided to become a comedian. But he's fascinated by medicine. His idea of a good time is to fly to the Mayo Clinic and watch operations. You think I'm kidding? One day he asked me to go with him. He said, "George, we'll have a great time. We'll see a couple of bypasses, a kidney transplant, a bowel resection. . . ." It was very tempting, but I had a good excuse for not going—I wasn't interested.

I'll never forget when Danny and Sylvia Kaye gave a party a few years ago. There were thirty or forty of us there, and after dinner a doctor who was one of the guests happened to mention a big flu epidemic going around and advised everyone to get flu shots. Well, that was all Danny had to hear. He made the doctor go out to his car and bring back his bag. Then we all had to roll up our sleeves, and while the doctor watched, Danny gave us the shots. And he did a pretty good job, too. I didn't catch the flu until I got home. I called Danny the next morning to find out what I should do about it. He said, "George, this is Wednesday," and hung up.

I'll say this for Dr. Kaye, he's one of our most talented stars, and when it comes to Chinese cooking there's nobody better. He's sort of a Jewish

Madame Wu. His noodles are always stiff. That's what Sylvia told me. And she's right—I've yet to eat at their house and get a soggy noodle. As a Chinese cook Danny's in a class by himself. And coming from me that's quite a compliment. I'm an expert on Chinese food. When I eat it I only use one chopstick.

Speaking of Chinese food, I must tell you about my operation. At my age I haven't got time to bother with transitions. When I was 78 I had a triple bypass. I wasn't going to have it, but my manager, Irving Fein, made such a good deal for me I couldn't turn it down.

It was a tough negotiation. My doctor started off by claiming I had a heart condition. But Irving said, "Wait a minute. How do we know it's a heart condition? Maybe it's only a little indigestion that will go away in a few days." The doctor answered, "If he's not operated on, *he'll* go away in a few days." Well, we lost that point.

The doctor told me I'd be in the hospital for two or three weeks, but I didn't want a booking for that long. I'd never played the room before, and I wasn't sure about the acoustics. So Irving settled for a three-day tryout with an option to renew.

The doctor wanted me in a private room, but Irving decided a semiprivate room was good enough. Actually I prefer a semiprivate room. As

Irving Fein and client.

long as I'm lying there I might as well have someone around to try out my routines on.

Well, we finally finished the negotations: a package deal, including surgery. And I must say Irving did a good job. He even got me top billing, right over EMERGENCY ROOM.

And the operation was a success. We had a good audience watching from the observation room above. After the doctor completed the triple bypass he got an ovation. In fact, he got so carried away he was tempted to do a fourth bypass for an encore. Fortunately, Danny Kaye was standing next to him and talked him out of it.

I don't want to tell you what the final bill was, but maybe this will give you a little hint. One of my friends was in the hospital for two days straight and it cost him $2,600. And he'd only come there to visit me.

I know I mentioned my operation in my last book, but I feel I have the right to talk about it again because this is a whole different routine. Oh, I forgot to tell you—while I was being operated on, Irving was up in the observation room selling autographed copies of my latest album.

Well, I've fooled around long enough. Now it's time to give you some profound, well-researched, carefully documented advice on this important subject. Since I don't know anyone who can do this for you, I'll have to try it myself.

When it comes to doctors there are many important decisions you have to make. The first is whether or not to have one. Some people say, "I haven't been sick for years, why do I need a doctor?" But the problem is, if you wait until you're really sick to go looking for a doctor, you're in real trouble. You have to make up your mind. You must either know a doctor or don't get sick. Face it, you have to use a little common sense. I can't make all your decisions. My advice is to have a doctor who knows your medical history, and while you're at it have the number of the nearest hospital or paramedic team in case of an emergency. Also make sure the liquor store delivers in case you're ever bedridden.

Finding the right doctor is very important, but it's not easy. It takes time and patience. Recommendations are a good start. So talk to your friends, preferably the ones who are still alive. Of course, some friends hate to recommend doctors. Talk to them anyway, they might give you the name of a good cleaning lady, or a good restaurant, or a shoe repair man. So you see, it's not a total loss; it doesn't hurt to ask. Come to think of it, my doctor was recommended to me by my shoe repair man.

If you've got the name of a doctor who sounds interesting, go to his office and check him out. Does he have medical books on his shelf among the investment and real estate volumes? Is the office tastefully done? Does he have an aquarium full of tropical fish? . . . Are the fish alive?

And look the doctor over. Does he look healthy? Does he seem to know what he's doing? See how he feels about being around sick people. Is he squeamish?

Then observe the patients in the waiting room. Do they look better than the fish? And talk to the patients. See what they think of him. And take out the doctor's wife a few times. See what she thinks of him. Find out if he makes house calls. If he does, send me his name. Also, determine if he takes credit cards, gives Green Stamps, or offers specials and discounts. And most important, does he validate parking?

You should think about whether you want an older doctor or a younger one. The younger ones are very energetic and more radical, up on all the new tricks. The older doctors don't need the new tricks. They've got an old trick up their sleeve. They know that ninety percent of your complaints will cure themselves. Personally, I like an older doctor. And if he's still alive, I ask who his doctor is and go to him . . . if he's still alive. As soon as I find a doctor my age I'm going to keep him.

You also want to decide whether you'll be more

comfortable with a male or female doctor. To me it doesn't make a bit of difference. I'm sure they both graduated from medical school and are equally qualified. And I don't mind taking my clothes off in front of a woman. What bothers me is having to pay her for it; I'm not used to that.

Even when you've found a doctor whom you like and have confidence in, remember: no matter what he or she advises, the final decision has to rest with you. About twenty years ago I went to this doctor who warned me to be more careful with the way I lived. He wanted me to cut out cigars, martinis, and women. He claimed I'd live longer. Who'd care to? He wanted me to eliminate anything around me that could kill me. So I got rid of the doctor. I probably added twenty years onto my life by doing that. Now I get a physical once a year from Danny Kaye and I feel great.

Author wanted to have his doctor in this picture, but it was taken on a Wednesday.

Stay Away From Funerals, Especially Yours

I HAVE FRIENDS around my age who get up in the morning, and the first thing they do is read the obituary column. If their name isn't in it, they have breakfast. Not me. I don't read the obituary column, I'm not interested in that kind of billing. If I did see my name in there, I'd still have breakfast. I'm not leaving on an empty stomach.

I don't know why people are so preoccupied with the obituaries. There's a lady in my neighborhood—I don't want to mention her name—who doesn't have any idea of what's going on in the world, but she's an expert on who just left it. She can tell you who died this morning, what he died of, what time he died, when and where the funeral is, and whether you should send flowers or a donation. She's always wearing black, and her eyes are red from crying. For her it's a dull week if she doesn't have a funeral or two to go to.

Author checking Obituary Column to see if he still
has his bridge game today.

I go to funerals. I pay my respects, I do all the things that are expected of me, but funerals don't happen to be my hobby. Those long processions have the right-of-way, and going through a red light makes me nervous. Not only that, but black isn't my favorite color, carnations make me sneeze, and I'm not crazy about organ music. Being a country singer . . . I like guitars.

To me, funerals are like bad movies. They last too long, they're overacted, and the ending is predictable. Another thing I don't understand about funerals: all the mourners show up in their somber clothes—black veils, black ties, black handkerchiefs. The deceased is the only one wearing a beige suit with a powder-blue shirt and a matching polka-dot tie. He looks great and we all look pathetic.

On the other hand, some funerals are beautifully done; the flowers, the music, the glowing eulogies. Sometimes they glow so much you're not sure whom they're talking about. I was at a funeral recently, and I happened to be sitting next to the widow and her young son. The minister gave this magnificent eulogy about the deceased. He praised his generosity, his nobility of spirit, what a devoted family man he was, what a caring husband, what a great provider—he went on and on. Finally, the widow leaned over to her son and whispered, "Go take a look and see if that's your father in there."

The King of Eulogies was Georgie Jessel. Nobody could move an audience like he could. He loved standing up there stirring our emotions, wringing out every tear. That was Jessel at his best. He'd rather be a smash at Forest Lawn than a hit at the London Palladium.

When Al Jolson died, Jessel took it for granted that he would do the eulogy. But twenty-four hours passed and nobody had called him. He became very concerned and telephoned his agent. The agent told him, "Georgie, I hate to tell you this, but I think they're going with somebody else."

Jessel said, "You've got to do something. I've been rehearsing his eulogy for hours, I've got it memorized. Nobody can put Jolie away like I can." He was so upset that he went over to see Mrs. Jolson. "Look," he said, "I've known Al all my life. What's the problem? Am I doing it or am I not?" She started to hesitate and Jessel said, "If I don't get to do Al's eulogy, I'll never speak to him again." Anyway, he did the eulogy and it was beautiful.

The next day at the club I saw him, and I said, "That eulogy you did at the mortuary for Jolson was so touching. You had us all crying like babies. You were just magnificent." Jessel said, "If you think that was something, you should have caught me at the grave."

Some years ago a well-known Broadway star

named Sam Bernard passed away, and of course Jessel did the eulogy. And Jessel loved Sam Bernard, so he really outdid himself. I ran into him five days later, and he was wearing his striped pants again, so I knew somebody else had died. Sure enough, he told me he was on his way to the mortuary to do a eulogy for Jim Barry. I said, "But, Georgie, how can you go down there and say nice things about him? You just told me at the Friars Club a few days ago that you hated Jim Barry." He said, "I know, but I've got some good stuff left over from Sam Bernard."

Here's a story Jessel used to tell. It's hard to believe, but he swore it was true. It seems there was this tap dancer, Joe Harris, who was really a great hoofer, and when he died Jessel gave the eulogy. The place was packed with all of Broadway's top dancers, and Jessel said, "If I must say so myself, it was one of my best eulogies. I was outstanding. But suddenly I got the shock of my life. Right in the middle of this beautiful tribute Joe Harris sat up in his coffin."

"My God, what did you do?" I asked.

Jessel answered, "What could I do—I sang a chorus of 'Strutter's Ball.'"

It was no accident that Jessel was such an expert at eulogies. He didn't wait for the people to die, he prepared ahead of time. I know he had my eulogy ready ten years ago. Every time I met him he'd say, "How do you feel?" I hated to tell him I felt fine; he'd get that hurt look on his face. And when I had my heart bypass he called me up in the hospital and said, "George, I'm pulling for you." I was worried; I didn't know which way he was pulling.

Whenever I met him at the club he was always trying out new lines on me for my eulogy. One day I was sitting there enjoying my lunch, minding my own business, and he came up to me, leaned over, and said, "George, you'll love this."

I said, "I know, that's why I ordered it. It's whitefish."

"No, no," Jessel said, "this new line I just thought of: 'As we're gathered here in this mossy glen, we recall with unashamed tears this scintillating straight man, this bulwark of show business, this cornucopia of wit, this—'"

"Georgie," I interrupted him, "cornucopia . . . I don't know what that means; I hate that word; I don't want that at my funeral."

He said, "What do you care—you won't hear it."

A couple of days later I was in the men's room and Jessel came up beside me and said, "George, you're right—cornucopia is out." I'd never had such exciting news in a bathroom before.

Another time I was in the middle of a bridge

game, and he pulled me aside. He said, "George, you've got to hear this."

"Georgie," I protested, "I've got an opening two-bid."

He said, "That can wait. This really flows: 'Let us not be misled by the departed's gruff speech and his gnarled countenance, for at this very moment, walking the streets out there is a five-year-old fatherless urchin to whom he'll always be the champ!'"

I looked at him. I couldn't believe it. "Georgie, you did that at Wallace Beery's funeral."

He nodded. "My boy, good stuff is timeless. And I've got some more good news for you: cornucopia is back in again!" I was so upset I went back to the table, played the hand, and went down three tricks.

This went on for years. One day I walked into the club and Jessel was sitting at the Round Table. I wasn't in the mood to listen to another highlight from my eulogy, so I turned around and left. But he came after me and jumped into my car just as I was about to drive away. He said, "George, this is so beautiful, if I wasn't your closest friend for sixty years, I wouldn't waste it on you."

"I knew I could count on you," I said.

"Pay attention! . . . 'As the shadows lengthen, we sit here basking in the warm and lugubrious memory of this magnificent blend of quality, this ambrosia of character that might never wend our way again, this—'"

"Hold it, hold it!" I said. "That's too flowery for me. I'm a simple man and I want it simple—plain words that get to the point."

He got out of the car and slammed the door. "For a guy who's gonna be just lying there, you're pretty fussy!" he said. And as I drove away, he hollered, "Drive carefully, I haven't finished your eulogy yet!" Poor Georgie—he never did. He got to his finish before he got to mine.

Well, I've treated a rather serious subject lightly. But I don't want to leave anybody with a wrong impression. I'm not out to ban funerals. I don't want the undertakers to hate me. I've got nothing against them. In fact, I once did a show at a morticians' convention and they were a very responsive audience. After all, how often do they get a chance to laugh?

But somewhere in this chapter I've tried to make a little point. The death of loved ones, friends, and acquaintances is something each of us faces and must deal with in his own way. And for most of us the funeral is part of this process. It's when people take it beyond its proper function that trouble starts. I don't think, for example, that a funeral was meant to be a test of the drawing power of the deceased. You hear things like: "How about that funeral they gave Charlie the other day. What a mob—the place was packed! There must have been fifteen hundred people there." With a crowd like that I'm surprised they had room for Charlie. If Charlie was going to do business like that, he should have played Vegas.

There are a lot of things like that about funerals that bother me. But maybe someday I'll change my mind. I change my mind about a lot of things. In fact, I changed it just now: I like "cornucopia."

There's Nothing More Important Than a Positive Attitude, I Think

HEY, that chapter title isn't bad. But the problem is, I'm locked in now and have to do a chapter on attitudes. I don't have a lot to say about attitudes. I didn't want to do a chapter on attitudes. But I thought of this clever title, so now I'm stuck with it. I wanted to do a chapter on the secrets of longevity but I didn't have a good title. And it would have been a great chapter because I have a lot of secrets I could tell. But you'll never hear them because I'm committed to attitudes. Okay, I'll write it, but I won't enjoy it. Well, here we go:

My dear readers, if you want to live to be over 100, you've got to have a positive attitude. If I say so myself, I have a positive attitude. I figure I'm 87 years old and I've had a wonderful life, and I see no reason why the next half shouldn't be as good. Anyway, I'm going to stick around and find out.

Let's take the other George. When he was freezing with his troops at Valley Forge, Pennsylvania, did Washington get discouraged? No. He said, "Men, it could be worse. We could all be freezing in New Jersey." With that positive attitude he went on to defeat the British, become our first President and one of our greatest Americans, even though he wasn't born on the Lower East Side like the rest of us. But you've got to respect the other George. He was a leader of men and a follower of women. (That line seems to call for a comment, or as we say in show business—a topper. Oh well, maybe I'll think of one after I've had my coffee.)

Then there was Ponce de Leon. He kept searching through the jungles of Florida, looking for the Fountain of Youth. Everybody told him it was a waste of time, but he kept on searching. He had a positive attitude right up to the day he died at the age of 26. I never understood Ponce very well. They give him credit for discovering Florida—but why shouldn't he discover it?—he was there anyway.

Some people never get discouraged. When General Custer was surrounded by all those Indians at Little Big Horn, did he worry and get gray hair over it? We'll never know—they never found his scalp.

Maybe the best example of a positive attitude was little David when he fought Goliath. Everybody told him he was crazy—Goliath would step on him, break him in half, chew him up and spit him out. The odds were 100 to 1 against David. Even his mother bet against him. But that didn't faze David. He knew he could take care of that big lummox with his little slingshot. And he did. The match was over before you knew it, and David's mother wouldn't talk to him for a week. But the point is, with that positive attitude, how could he lose? On the other hand, Goliath had just as positive an attitude. How come he lost? Why did I bring that up? It confuses the whole issue.

I still know one thing: it doesn't hurt to have a positive attitude. Even if you're going to fail, be positive about it. That way you'll be a successful failure.

Another attitude I'm in favor of is thinking young. As they get older, too many people tend to hang around with each other and compare ailments and gravy stains. That might be fun, but it's good to mix with younger people, too. I love being around young people. I figure maybe some of that youth will rub off on me. And maybe some of what I've got might rub off on them; that is, if it doesn't drop off before I meet them.

Some older people get depressed around young people. It reminds them of how young they used to be themselves. Not me. I look at those young people

Wrong attitude.

Right attitude.

and see how young I still am. There's only one thing they can do better than I can. Well, maybe not better, just more often.

The idea is to keep a young mind and a healthy body. I have a young mind, and I'm taking a healthy body to the Bistro for dinner tonight.

Look, I don't want anyone to get the idea that I don't like old people. I love old people. Some of my best friends were old. Let me clear something up for you. When I say I *think* young, it doesn't mean I'm trying to *be* young. I'm not trying to be an 18-year-old, or even a 20-year-old. I don't wear tight jeans. If I did, it would only be to help me stand up. And I don't go surfing. Until the other day I thought "hang 10" was a Chinese restaurant. I don't cruise Hollywood Boulevard Friday nights. To me a cruise is ten days on the S.S. *Leviathan*. Who am I kidding? My hair is gray. If I wanted black hair, I'd buy it that way.

When I talk about thinking young, I'm talking about enthusiasm, keeping active, having plans, projects for tomorrow, meeting people, doing things; I look to the future, because that's where I'm going to spend the rest of my life. A lot of people are too quick to decide that their life is over. And if you really think your life is over, and you have no place to go, I advise you to take very short steps. It'll take you longer to get there.

I feel sorry for people who live in the past. I know it was cheaper then, and I know that some people had very interesting pasts, but you can't keep looking in a rearview mirror—unless you enjoy having a stiff neck. Old memories are fine, but you've still got time to make new memories.

I don't live in the past, I live in a house in Beverly Hills. It's more comfortable. Actually, you may not believe this, but it's true. I don't surround myself with memorabilia. I don't waste time looking through scrapbooks of my career or rereading my old reviews—they were painful enough to read the first time. I don't even watch my old movies. I'm not interested in what happened yesterday, I find it's best to fall in love with what you're doing today. The things I did yesterday I was in love with yesterday. But that romance is over. I'm very fickle.

When people get a little older they are frightened to make a change in their lives. It's easier to stay in that same safe rut. To me that challenge is exciting. Some of the things I didn't want to do turned out to be the best things I ever did. At 79 I became a dramatic actor and did *The Sunshine Boys*, and at 81 I played "God." In fact, I made two "God" pictures. If they make another one and will pay me, I'll be glad to come down again. When I was 84 Charlie Fach of Mercury Records came to me with a country song called "I Wish I Was 18

Again" and wanted me to sing it. I said to him, "I was born in New York, I've got a New York accent, I can't be a country singer." Then Charlie told me how much they were going to pay me and I said, "Pardner, I've got a hankerin' to sing your lil ole song." Then I moseyed down and signed the contract. I'm happy to say the song turned out to be a hit even though I had never hankered before. I just finished my third country album, and as long as they play in my key I'll keep on hankerin'. I'm getting so country I might even buy myself a spread like those other country singers. And I might even get myself three or four hundred head of cattle. If I like the heads, I'll get the bodies to go with them. Look, when I hanker, I hanker.

There's an old saying, "Life begins at 40." That's silly—life begins every morning when you wake up. Old sayings . . . why are the sayings always old? Like "Life is just a bowl of cherries"—why aren't there new sayings? I think I'll make up a new saying: "Life is just a bowl of tangerines."

Oh yeah—remember at the early part of the chapter where I did a line about George Washington, and I couldn't think of a topper because I hadn't had my coffee? Well, I just had my coffee, and here's the line and the topper: "He was a leader of men and a follower of women." Which is better than being a leader of women and a follower of men. . . . Well, the coffee wasn't so hot either.

Okay, back to attitude. Just because you're old it doesn't mean you can't lead a full, vigorous, and active life. Open your mind to it, don't just sit there—do things. Swim the English Channel; find a cure for the common cold; be the first to go over Niagara Falls in a rocking chair; think of some new old sayings. You see, the possibilities are endless.

If all else fails, try doing something nice for somebody who doesn't expect it. You'll be surprised how good you'll feel. The Boy Scouts have the right idea. Many's the time I've helped a young lady across the street and over to my place. You should see all my merit badges.

The point is, with a good positive attitude and a little bit of luck, there's no reason you can't live to be 100. Once you've done that you've really got it made, because very few people die over 100.

Wait, I Just Thought of Something

WHEN I'M ON the stage the only thing I'm interested in is getting laughs. That's all they expect of me and it's all I worry about. But being an author is something else again. Authors have to be responsible for what they say. It concerns me that I may have given some wrong information, made a few errors here and there. It's keeping me up nights. Well, I wouldn't say it keeps me up nights, but it interferes with my naps. See what I mean? I just made a remark I had to correct. What if there are other things I've missed? An author has a conscience, you know. I could correct every mistake I've made, but that would mean reading through the whole book, and I'm not that upset.

Come to think of it, I do remember a few things. In my chapter on diets I stated that my Monday breakfast consisted of four prunes. That's wrong.

181

I remember one Monday when I was very hungry and I ate five.

I also seem to remember saying that Ponce de Leon died at 26. I was a few years off. He died at 61. But at 61, I would have had no joke. Now I'm sorry I didn't have him die at 24.

And when I said that Georgie Jessel and I were standing in the men's room, that was wrong, too. We weren't standing, we were sitting.

Also, I think I've left you with the impression that I'm always going out with young girls. That's not true, either. Sometimes I stay home with them.

As long as I'm setting the record straight, this is really going to shock you—I did not write this book alone! I had four collaborators: Hal Goldman, Fred Fox, Seaman Jacobs, and Harvey Berger, without whose constant help, creative guidance, and numerous contributions this book might have been a lot better.

And don't be fooled by the photograph of my writers—they're not that funny. Harvey—the one who looks a little like William Penn—I've never worked with before. But the other three have been with me for years . . . so with them I should have known better.

Actually, I'm very fond of those three guys. They're nice fellows and they have a wonderful sense of humor. They laugh at everything I say. I'll

tell you the truth, the real reason these three writers are still with me is they sing harmony. I know I should say a few more things about Harvey, but he asked me not to.

Incidentally, if by some outside chance, after reading this book you don't live to be 100, don't sue me, sue my writers—they're very rich.

There are many others I should acknowledge: Irving Fein, my manager, who's married to Marion Fein, his manager. Irving was invaluable to this project. I can't tell you how many times he stuck his head into our office and asked, "How's it going, fellows?" In this organization everyone contributes in his own way.

Then there's Jack Langdon, my secretary, who typed every page of this book, and who's been with me for thirty years . . . and that's about all I can say about him.

And I certainly have to say something about my literary agent, Arthur Pine. I suggested that he wait for his commission until I reach 100, because money would be worth more then. But not caring about the value of money, he said he'd rather have it right now. Arthur is a fine literary agent, but he's not too bright about money.

Now I want to thank our photographer, who did the front and back covers and most of the pic-

Author with Oscar. This has nothing to do with the book, but for an ending it looks impressive.

tures in the book, Mr. Peter C. Borsari. The C stands for "click."

The three charming girls who did the exercises are: Stephanie Black, Tonya McCollom, and Jo Connell. Their combined measurements are— 102-72-102.

The attractive young actor and actress in the chapter on worry, stress, and tension are Jeff Severson and Dorit Stevens. You'll be seeing Jeff in pictures soon, and I expect to see Dorit next Tuesday night.

And I certainly have to mention Daniel and Arlette D'Hoore, the very competent couple who work for me. She stews my prunes and he serves them.

I wouldn't forgive myself if I didn't mention Robert Redford, Elizabeth Taylor, Cary Grant, Bo Derek, Frank Sinatra, Cathy Carr, Walter Matthau, Katharine Hepburn, Jack Lemmon, Helen Hayes, Sammy Davis, Cathy Carr, Burt Reynolds, Dolly Parton, Fred Astaire, Lucille Ball, Bob Hope, Cathy Carr, Gregory Peck, and Carol Channing.

These famous names have nothing to do with the book. That's why I mentioned them at the end. If I mentioned them at the beginning, I'd have to say something about them.

However, you'll notice Cathy Carr was mentioned three times. She happens to be a very close friend of the author's.

Last, but definitely not least, I want to thank Phyllis Grann, my editor and publisher, who also happens to be a beautiful lady. Now that I'm working for her, I hope I can interest her in the benefits of sexual harassment.

More Biography and Autobiography from SIGNET

Buy them at your local

bookstore or use coupon

on next page for ordering.